570

FRIENDS
OF ACPL

D1269276

Haiti

in pictures

By KEN WEDDLE

VISUAL
GEOGRAPHY
SERIES

 STERLING PUBLISHING CO., INC. NEW YORK

Oak Tree Press Co., Ltd. London & Sydney

VISUAL GEOGRAPHY SERIES

Afghanistan
Alaska
Argentina
Australia
Austria
Belgium and Luxembourg
Berlin—East and West
Bolivia
Brazil
Bulgaria
Canada
The Caribbean (English-
  Speaking Islands)
Ceylon (Sri Lanka)
Chile
China
Colombia
Costa Rica
Cuba
Czechoslovakia
Denmark
Ecuador
Egypt
El Salvador
England

Ethiopia
Fiji
Finland
France
French Canada
Ghana
Greece
Greenland
Guatemala
Haiti
Hawaii
Holland
Honduras
Hong Kong
Hungary
Iceland
India
Indonesia
Iran
Iraq
Ireland
Islands of the
  Mediterranean
Israel
Italy

Jamaica
Japan
Jordan
Kenya
Korea
Kuwait
Lebanon
Liberia
Madagascar (Malagasy)
Malawi
Malaysia and Singapore
Mexico
Morocco
Nepal
New Zealand
Nicaragua
Norway
Pakistan and Bangladesh
Panama and the Canal
  Zone
Peru
The Philippines
Poland
Portugal
Puerto Rico

Rhodesia
Rumania
Russia
Saudi Arabia
Scotland
Senegal
South Africa
Spain
Surinam
Sweden
Switzerland
Tahiti and the
  French Islands of
  the Pacific
Taiwan
Tanzania
Thailand
Tunisia
Turkey
Uruguay
The U.S.A.
Venezuela
Wales
West Germany
Yugoslavia

PICTURE CREDITS

The publishers wish to thank the following for use of photographs in this book: Jean-Claude Bordes, Haitian Tourist Bureau, New York; Charles Georges, Haitian Tourist Bureau, Port-au-Prince; Nathan A. Haverstock, The Latin American Service, Washington, D.C.; United Nations; Ken Weddle.

Copyright © 1974 by Sterling Publishing Co., Inc.
419 Park Avenue South, New York, N.Y. 10016
British edition published by Oak Tree Press Co., Ltd., Nassau, Bahamas
Distributed in Australia and New Zealand by Oak Tree Press Co., Ltd.,
P.O. Box J34, Brickfield Hill, Sydney 2000, N.S.W.
Distributed in the United Kingdom and elsewhere in the British Commonwealth
by Ward Lock Ltd., 116 Baker Street, London W 1
Manufactured in the United States of America
All rights reserved
Library of Congress Catalog Card No.: 73–93603
Sterling ISBN 0–8069–1182–4 Trade   Oak Tree 7061–2495–2
1183-2 Library

Plying between Port-au-Prince and Carrefour is the tourists' delight, the "Tap-Tap." These brightly painted Haitian "buses" charge minimal fares. They are built locally by mounting bus bodies on pick-up truck frames. The name is derived from the sound of the Diesel engine.

CONTENTS

NO. SCHOOL
C823373

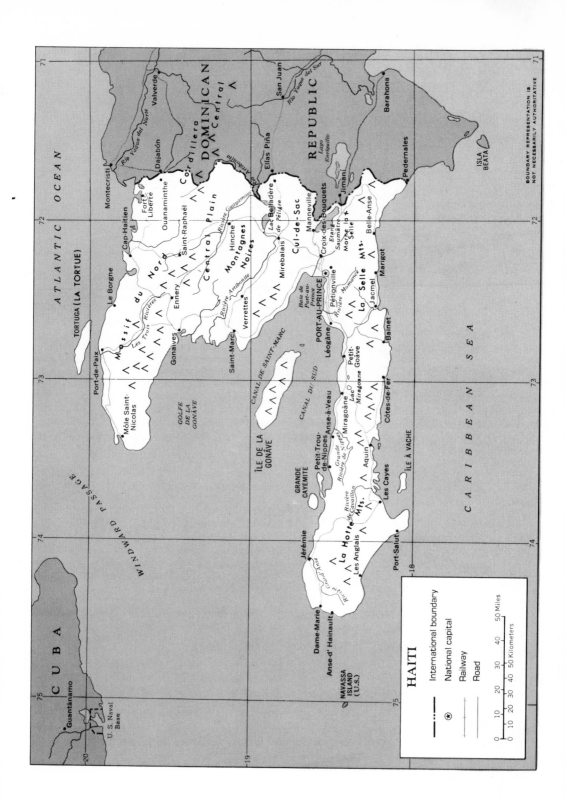

HAITI

- ·-·-· International boundary
- ⊛ National capital
- Railway
- Road

0   10   20   30   40   50 Miles
0 10 20 30 40 50 Kilometers

Haiti means "High Land" in the Arawak tongue. Indeed, three fourths of the Republic's total area is mountainous, with high valleys where peasant farmers toil for a slender living.

I. THE LAND

OFTEN REFERRED to as the Black Republic, Haiti occupies the western third of the island of Hispaniola, which lies about 50 miles southeast of Cuba in the great archipelago called the Antilles or the West Indies, with the Atlantic Ocean on the north and the Caribbean Sea on the west and south. The eastern two-thirds are occupied by the Dominican Republic and the boundary line between the two independent nations is about 193 miles (309 km.) long, following an irregular mountainous course from north to south.

On the map Haiti resembles the yawning mouth of a huge sea monster, with its two large peninsulas enclosing the Gulf of Gonâve. Port-au-Prince, Haiti's capital, lies approximately 700 air miles (1,120 km.) southeast of Miami or about 1,365 miles (2,184 km.) due south from New York City. With an area of 10,714 square miles (27,750 sq. km.) Haiti is about twice the size of Northern Ireland and somewhat larger than Vermont.

The sun-drenched island commands a strategic location along the major trade routes be-

Along the narrow roads of Haiti, one may come across sparkling mountain waterfalls such as this one, overhung by a foot bridge.

tween Europe and the Isthmus of Panama and between the North American east coast and Latin America. About 100 miles (160 km.) due west of its southern peninsula is the island of Jamaica, and about 30 miles (48 km.) off, also due west, is the small island of Navassa, belonging to the United States. Near the coast are several islands belonging to Haiti, chief of which are Gonâve and Tortuga.

TOPOGRAPHY

Haiti, so named by the Taino Indians, means "High Land," and lives up to its name, for three fourths of Haiti's area is very mountainous with peaks soaring to as high as 8,700 feet (2,654 metres). The coastline is as jagged as the mountain tops with many deep indentations forming excellent ports.

The country has three main mountain ranges —one runs east and west along the southern peninsula, while the others stretch northwestward across the mainland. The principal mountain range on Hispaniola is the Cordillera Central which extends from the Dominican Republic into northeastern Haiti. In the middle of the country are the Montagnes Noires and along the southern coast are the range called the Massif de la Hotte and its eastern continuation, the Massif de la Selle. Generally speaking,

the mountains are not as high as those of the Dominican Republic. Haiti's highest peak is Morne la Selle, in the southeast, which reaches 8,790 feet (2,681 metres).

Lonely lighthouses, such as this one between Port-de-Paix and Cap-Haïtien, protect shipping along the rugged northern coastline of Haiti.

6

Parts of Haiti, especially in the south, are arid and rather sparsely wooded.

Between the mountains and along their outer fringes lie several plains. The Artibonite and Cul-de-Sac Plains, fan out from the Gulf of Gonâve toward the interior, while the Central Plain is a large interior plain that touches the Dominican border. To the north the North Plain stretches along the northern coast between the mountains and the sea. About 85 per cent of Haiti's population is concentrated in the agricultural regions of the great plains and valleys.

Rushing streams spring from the mountain slopes forming numerous short rivers that cascade into the sea. Only one river, the Artibonite, is navigable and has a large dam for irrigation and hydro-electric purposes, creating the artificial lake called Lac du Péligre.

There are two natural lakes, the largest of which is Etang Saumâtre, covering about 43 square miles (111 sq. km.), situated east of Port-au-Prince. The lake has no apparent outlet to the sea and the water is slightly salty.

Near the middle of the southern peninsula is Lac Miragoane, a fresh-water lake of about 10 square miles (26 sq. km.) that empties into the sea.

CLIMATE

Caressed by the soft tradewinds of the Atlantic, Haiti enjoys a tropical marine climate all year round. The temperature of the main seaports of the nation range on an average from 68° to 94°F. (20° to 34°C.), with but an 8° to 10° difference between summer and winter. Temperatures take a decided dip with increases of altitude, and in the lofty mountains it is cool and pleasant, like eternal spring. Thus, Port-au-Prince the capital, only 120 feet (36 metres) above sea-level, has an approximate yearly average temperature of 80°F. (26°C.), while Furcy, only a short distance away with an altitude of 5,000 feet (1,525 metres) above

It is the dry season and no water runs in the bed of this stream in the hills near Port-au-Prince. Local and United Nations forestry experts are checking the area for erosion.

NATURAL RESOURCES

Haiti, like many other islands dotting the blue Caribbean, has only a limited amount of mineral resources. Bauxite, an ore from which aluminium is extracted, is mined commercially, but many minerals have not as yet been fully developed. Among the undeveloped resources are gold, silver, antimony, tin, sulphur, coal, nickel, gypsum and porphyry. All subsoil rights belong to the state. Private gold mining is permitted but the metal must be sold to the National Bank of the Republic. Exploration and drilling for oil is just getting started, but so far has not been very rewarding. Meanwhile, bauxite, copper, lignite (brown coal) and manganese continue to be mined in limited amounts for export.

FLORA AND FAUNA

Entering Haiti is like entering a vast greenhouse of exotic blooming flowers. Tourists, especially those from colder climates, are fascinated to see the most unusual and expensive

sea-level, has a yearly average temperature reading of close to 61°F. (16°C.).

Because of the slight variation in temperature, Haitians think of their seasons as the dry and rainy periods. There are two rainy seasons, from April to June and from October to November. Rains fall in a regular pattern almost every day of the rainy season, but the rain is not a continuous downpour as one might imagine. Rarely does Haiti have a grey day when the sun does not shine. Showers fall in spells by the bucketful, but they stop as suddenly as they begin and the island is soon dry again, with bright colors and rainbows.

On the side of bad weather are the seasonal hurricanes. Located near the point in the Caribbean where tropical storms seem to breed, Haiti has all too often been battered by devastating blows of nature. During the "Big Blow" of 1963, when hurricane Flora swept over the island, more than 3,000 persons lost their lives, making it one of the worst storms in the island's history. The hurricane season lasts from June through October with July, August and September the most dangerous months. While most Haitians fear the big winds, they accept the perils of nature as a part of island life.

Travellers make their way through the vast pine forest which lies about 60 miles (96 km.) east of Port-au-Prince in the mountains near the Dominican border.

The Harry Truman Boulevard in Port-au-Prince is shaded by graceful palms.

of exotic hot-house plants growing in wild profusion all over the island. Orchids in all their tropical beauty literally tumble from the trees in great flowering clusters.

Another blossom for which Haiti is famous is the royal poinciana. The sight of these huge flame-hued flowers against the brilliant blue of the Caribbean sky is alone well worth a visit to Haiti. Next in popularity to the royal poinciana is the fragrant frangipani with its soft, velvety blossoms, shaped like a star, that may be red, pink, yellow or creamy white. The blossoms fill the air with a strong sweet fragrance, but once picked, they fade quickly and soon become evil-smelling.

In addition to the wonderful world of flowers, Haiti can justly boast of its wide variety of palm trees, the most stately of which is the royal palm towering up to 60 feet (18 metres). These giants lend an air of elegance to many of the wide avenues of Port-au-Prince, while the graceful coconut palms line many of the island's long waterfronts and unspoiled beaches.

High in the upper mountain ranges the rain forest produces pines, ferns, mahogany, cedar, and rosewood. Many of the island trees are as pleasing to the palate as they are to the eye. Among the edible fruits are the avocado, the mango, breadfruit, sapodilla, orange, guava, papaya and banana. Coffee, cocoa, coconut and many of the tropical fruit trees often grow in wild confusion along the lower mountain edges.

Although Haiti has approximately 150,000 acres (60,750 hectares) of excellent pine forest, primitive forestry practices as well as tree disease have drastically reduced timber production. Haitian pine found in the northern mountains is high in turpentine and rosin, and there the processing of turpentine and rosin are important industries. Lignum vitae stands on the otherwise barren island of Gonâve and on the northwest mainland are of considerable extent, but continuous cutting and stripping to make charcoal and provide firewood has reduced them so that only small amounts are now suitable for export. Lignum vitae is valued for shipbuilding and for butcher's blocks.

As with most Caribbean islands, Haiti has its share of insects, scorpions, spiders and centipedes, but there are no large wild animals or poisonous snakes. The inland lakes provide a sanctuary for many beautiful egrets, flamingoes, migrating ducks and small tropical birds. Reptile life includes several varieties of crocodiles, rhino-horned iguanas and small lizards that live on insects.

An important resource that remains virtually untouched is commercial fishing. Haiti is directly in the path of major fish migrations and offshore waters abound in tuna, marlin, bonito, tarpon, bass and rock lobster. However, Haitian fishermen seldom venture more than a few miles from their home ports for want of more modern fishing equipment and trustworthy fishing boats. The total annual catch, estimated at nearly 5,000,000 pounds (2,268,000 kilos) is caught with the simplest type fishing gear. The inland waters also provide a source of good edible food, but lack of transport and modern facilities limit this important food source for sale to local consumption.

Much of Haiti has been denuded by unrestrictive wood cutting, creating serious erosion. This area was once part of a pine forest.

Jérémie, "The City of Poets," lies 70 miles (112 km.) from Les Cayes, on the north shore of the southern peninsula. General Alexandre Dumas, the father and grandfather of the great French writers of the same name, was born here. Founded in 1756, the city is famous for natural beauty and the great variety of tropical fruit grown nearby, as well as for its excellent beach. The heart of the city is Alexandre Square (seen here) with its lovely church and palm trees.

CITIES

Nearly all of the major cities of Haiti are located on broad, deep bays and serve as ports open to foreign commerce. Port-au-Prince, on the easternmost point of the Gulf of Gonâve is the national capital and largest city with an estimated 350,000 inhabitants. Cap-Haïtien, a seaport on the northern coast is Haiti's second largest city with about 25,000 people. Among the other cities and large towns of regional importance are Jérémie and Les Cayes on the southern peninsula, Port-de-Paix on the northern peninsula, and Saint Marc and Gonaïves which are both located on the Gulf of Gonâve, all with populations considerably under 25,000.

PORT-AU-PRINCE

Port-au-Prince is the heart of Haiti—a city of endless contrasts. It is a place of sounds —church bells tolling at 4 A.M., vendors hawking their wares, murmuring voices—and smells —fruit, frangipani blossoms, spices, salt air and the scent of fish that all seaports seem to have.

The buildings of the city vary from dazzling white government offices to antiquated, gingerbread structures built before the turn of the

The crowded Iron Market, chief market for foods and goods in Port-au-Prince, is named for its sheet-iron gate flanked by Oriental towers, erected in 1889 by President Florvil Hyppolite.

It is feeding time for the pigeons in one of the beautiful city parks in Port-au-Prince.

In the Iron Market at Port-au-Prince one can buy gaily patterned fabrics from one vendor and have them made into articles of clothing by a seamstress, all under the same roof.

century. Unpaved streets with cobblestone sidewalks run into wide, modern paved avenues where gleaming Cadillacs compete for the right of way with braying donkeys laden with green vegetables headed for the city market.

Even more interesting are the people—there are few white faces here but brown and black faces everywhere. Straight-backed women with baskets loaded with greenery head for the city market during the day, while at night the flickering glow of the charcoal fires of street vendors light up the warm humid air like a million fireflies on the wing, and the thumping of voodoo drums sweep in from the hills.

Everywhere there is poverty, yet this black metropolis is not a depressing slum, but rather a place full of life and warmth. The city is built in tiers above the sparkling blue waters of the bay, gradually leading up to the fashionable resort area of the capital known as Pétionville. Here in the cool of the scenic mountains with a panoramic view of the blue waters of the port are the homes of many of Haiti's mulattoes.

CAP-HAÏTIEN

Over 5 hours by road and only 45 minutes by plane from the capital, Cap-Haïtien, Haiti's second largest city, is the jumping-off point for exploring the famous Sans Souci Palace and Citadelle of Henri Christophe. Located at the foot of the lime-green mountains of the north

Construction work on a new building in downtown Port-au-Prince continues at a slow pace because of the lack of modern building equipment.

13

coast, this picturesque little city recalls Haiti's turbulent past. Once known as the Paris of the Antilles, this was the city of the black Emperor Henri Christophe. Cap-Haïtien is perhaps the most beautiful city in all of Haiti, as well as the most historical, and is fast developing as a tourist hub and cruise ship port.

The handful of small towns scattered along Haiti's coastline holds very little interest for the average traveller. Many of the places are inaccessible by roads and may be reached only by muleback or foot. This is voodoo country, where it is better to stick to the beaten path.

Cap-Haïtien is a city rich in history. The city, first called Le Cap, then Cap Français, then Cap-Henri, and finally Cap-Haïtien, with 35,000 people, is today Haiti's second largest city. Its domed cathedral can be seen at the upper right.

The shell of the Palace of Sans Souci at Milot is all that remains of King Henri Christophe's most elaborate residence. It had marble floors, mahogany walls, grand stairways and an underground stream beneath it.

2. HISTORY

HISTORICALLY, the bitter and sometimes romantic story of Haiti begins at dusk on the evening of December 5th, 1492, when a lookout atop Christopher Columbus's ship, the "Pinta," shouted "Tierra! Tierra!" (Land! Land!). Waiting for the light of dawn the explorer then selected a fine bay and anchored the Santa Maria, preparatory to going ashore. Because it was the feast day of St. Nicholas, Columbus named the beautiful port for that Saint—the place is today called Môle St. Nicolas. Later as he cruised eastward along the northern coast he named the beautiful island La Isla Espânola (the Spanish isle), later corrupted to Hispaniola.

Although the great explorer was disappointed that Hispaniola did not prove to be China or India as he had anticipated, he nevertheless quickly succumbed to the beauty of the island and the friendliness of the brown-skinned natives who greeted him. In time the island was to become known as the "land Columbus loved best." In fulfilment of his dying request his body now rests in the ornate cathedral at Santo Domingo, in the Dominican Republic.

A statue of Christopher Columbus, who discovered Haiti on his first voyage in 1492, overlooks the bay at Port-au-Prince.

THE ARAWAKS

Making landfall again near what is today Cap-Haïtien, Columbus was greeted by the natives, who showered him with gifts of lush, ripe fruit, and other food, tobacco and trinkets of gold. They called themselves "Tainos," (the Good People) and their lovely island "Hayti," meaning the mountainous country. The aborigines were of the Arawak tribe, a gentle, peaceful people, who occupied most of the larger islands of the Caribbean at the time. Columbus noted that the Arawaks were an extremely graceful and handsome people who wore their soft black hair in a style similar to the Spanish mode of the day, and due to the delightful climate, they wore a minimum of clothing. Most of all, Columbus much admired the comfortable hammocks of the natives made of sisal fibre which he soon adopted for use aboard his ships.

16

THE FIRST SETTLEMENT

Fate was soon to play an unscheduled part in the history of the world when, three weeks later, on Christmas day, the Santa Maria was wrecked on the beautiful but treacherous coral reefs at the entrance of Acule Bay, near present-day Cap-Haïtien. Again the Arawaks demonstrated their friendliness by salvaging the wreck and carrying the heavy timbers ashore, from which Columbus built a wooden fort and founded the first settlement in the New World on Christmas day, 1492. He named the settlement La Villa de la Navidad, or, Town of the Nativity. Historically, it marked the first settlement by white men in the Western Hemisphere.

HISPANIOLA DESERTED

The Arawaks, together with the first settlers were soon to become extinct. Another tribe of Indians were pushing north from South America in their long dugout canoes. They were a fierce and warlike tribe, whom the Arawaks called "Carib," the word meaning "cannibal" in the Arawak language. The fierce Caribs killed and enslaved the Arawaks until they were soon the undisputed rulers of Hispaniola.

Meanwhile, Columbus had returned to Spain where he was busy organizing a large expeditionary force for the purpose of colonizing the New World he had just discovered. Leaving the Spanish port of Cadiz in September, 1493, with a large fleet of 17 sailing vessels and 1,200 people, the navigator made all haste to return to the first settlement of Navidad. There to his bitter disappointment he found that the original settlers had been massacred by the Caribs and the fort burned to the ground.

Saddened, but undaunted, the admiral sailed his fleet farther east along the north coast and established a new settlement, which failed to take hold because of the unhealthy climate. In 1496, the settlement was moved to a much healthier and better location on the south coast of Hispaniola, now the city of Santo Domingo. The Caribs were gradually subdued, and for the first half of the 16th century, the island of Hispaniola flourished, not for what the land

After the Santa Maria went down off Cap-Haïtien, the ship's anchor was retrieved and now is a leading exhibit at the National Museum in Port-au-Prince.

produced, but because it served as an ideal base for the expeditions of the Spanish conquistadors to explore and conquer other nearby lands in their relentless pursuit of gold and silver.

Meanwhile, with the discovery of gold in Mexico and Peru, Hispaniola suddenly lost its appeal, as Europeans rushed to the more attractive mainland where gold and silver were to be found. By this time all that remained of the friendly Arawaks were broken pottery and memories of their haunting music. The fierce Caribs were also fighting for their very lives under the punishing lashes of cruel overseers, who forced them to work in the mines for gold until they dropped in their tracks from exhaustion. By 1550, Hispaniola had been almost abandoned. There was relatively little silver or gold to be found and so the colony was of very little value to the Spanish crown.

FRENCH BUCCANEERS

With the discovery of gold in Mexico and Peru, the Caribbean Sea became a busy shipping lane for treasure-laden galleons sailing home to Spain. By the year 1630, the island of Tortuga—off the north coast of Haiti—had been settled by French and British adventurers, better known as buccaneers. Using the small island as a rendezvous, the pirates would sail forth to terrorize and plunder the Spanish merchant fleets filled with riches seized from the Aztec and Inca empires. Within a short time the freebooters had established a firm hold on the nearby mainland, at Cap-Haïtien.

Spain was unable to cope with the widespread seizure of land by the ruthless pirates, and ceded the western one-third of the island to France under the treaty of Ryswick in 1697.

In the early 1600's, French and English pirates began to settle on the small island of Tortuga (La Tortue) just off the northern coast of Hispaniola. Today a few old cannons and other remains are all that is left to recall those bloodthirsty days.

owners and 27,000 mulattoes (or mixtures of white and negro stock). Although the mulattoes were free men, their rights were severely restricted by racial laws. Among them, some were very wealthy, owners of large plantations and many slaves, arousing the dislike and jealousy of the white plantation owners. Cruel mistreatment of the slaves and the humiliation inflicted upon the mulattoes by the whites led to frequent revolts, and unhealed scars still exist today. Wretched, poor, overworked and undernourished, the weary slaves could only wait for the day of reckoning.

THE SLAVE REVOLT

In 1791, two important events set the stage for Haiti's ultimate independence. One was the French Revolution, which led the mulattoes of Haiti to believe they could gain social and racial equality with the white class, by calling for new laws and social legislation. The other was a violent uprising of the slaves in the north that swiftly spread throughout the nation. Thousands of colonists were massacred, plantation homes burned to the ground and the wealth-producing sugar industry of the nation was totally destroyed. Although the slaves suffered strong reprisals (an estimated 20,000 died), their hopes for freedom were never crushed. During the violence many plantation owners and mulattoes fled the nation, never to return.

Weakened by the French Revolution and unable to send sufficient armed forces to quell the uprising, France was forced to grant the slaves their freedom in 1793. Taking advantage of these chaotic conditions, Spain and England started moving their armies in to claim the burned-out plantations and the French found that they were faced with serious problems from all directions.

This left the eastern two-thirds of the island (now the Dominican Republic) under Spanish control. France named its new possession Saint Domingue, but today it is known as the Republic of Haiti.

FRENCH COLONIAL PERIOD

Under French rule the new possession started to prosper almost from the very beginning. French settlers using black slaves brought from Africa lost no time in establishing vast plantations for agricultural purposes. In the dry areas, such as the Cul-de-Sac, the colonists forced the slaves to erect a vast network of irrigation systems to water the fields. As the 17th century drew to a close, it was clear that the future economy of the French colony would depend upon sugar, rum and slaves. As the colony continued to prosper, so did the demand for more and more slaves.

By the close of the 18th century, St. Domingue had a population consisting of about half a million black slaves, 30,000 white plantation

Jean-Jacques Dessalines (1758-1806) defeated Napoleon's superior army and proclaimed Haiti's independence.

A QUARTET OF HEROES

For a better understanding of the turbulent years to follow it is best to become acquainted with four of Haiti's famous heroes. Toussaint L'Ouverture (1743–1803) was a black general who paved the way for the freedom of the slaves. Jean-Jacques Dessalines (1758–1806) was the black George Washington of Haiti, who defeated Napoleon's army and proclaimed Haiti's independence. Alexandre Sabes Pétion (1770–1818), a mulatto, was the first president of a republic established in southern Haiti. Henri Christophe (1767–1820), king of northern Haiti from 1811–20, built the famous Citadel and the Palace of Sans Souci.

TOUSSAINT L'OUVERTURE

Although the slaves in 1793 had their freedom, 12 more years of bloody fighting continued, until out of the chaos, Toussaint L'Ouverture emerged to become the first of Haiti's great liberators and national heroes. L'Ouverture, an ex-slave who had worked his way up through the ranks to become a general in the French army, managed to gather a small ragged black army from the interior and successfully drove out the Spanish and English invaders who were rapidly taking over the devastated sugar plantations. He established peace and drafted a constitution that permanently abolished slavery. In turn Toussaint was installed as the Governor General of Saint Domingue for life.

He put the peasants back to work on the plantations under military rule and attempted to repair some of the damage caused by the long years of warfare. Firmly entrenched as the ruler of Saint Domingue, he began a campaign to rid the entire island of Hispaniola of slavery. By 1801, he had captured the Spanish city of

The black general, Toussaint L'Ouverture (1743-1803), paved the way for freedom of the slaves.

19

INDEPENDENCE

Enraged over the betrayal that had placed their leader in chains, three army generals who had fought under the leadership of Toussaint—Henri Christophe, Dessalines and Pétion—kept the fire of rebellion blazing, by uniting their black followers and resuming the war against the forces of Napoleon with more determination than ever. The object of the war which the blacks now waged was to abolish slavery forever and to declare their independence from France. The French, greatly weakened by an outbreak of yellow fever, after a year of bitter fighting, finally surrendered on November 18, 1803, to General Dessalines.

France had lost its richest colony—and with it the staging area for Napoleon's bold plans to rule North America. As a result the United States was never invaded as Napoleon had

Santo Domingo, capital of the old Spanish colony, where he abolished slavery and established a new government with himself as head.

NAPOLEON

Although Toussaint L'Ouverture did not proclaim the independence of the island, his action of freeing the slaves met with strong objections from the French government. Napoleon Bonaparte, not wanting to lose the rich colony, then sent a huge army under the command of General Charles Leclerc, with orders to subdue Toussaint and restore slavery throughout the colony just as it had existed before the violent slave rebellion. Against such odds, Toussaint's resistance was short-lived. Toussaint was captured while negotiating peace under a flag of truce and was sent to France where he died in prison on April 7, 1803.

Alexandre Sabes Pétion (1770-1818), a mulatto, was first president of the republic established in southern Haiti.

An old print shows the crowning of Henri Christophe as King of (northern) Haiti.

planned, and he sold the vast Louisiana Territory to the United States for a mere U.S. $15,000,000.

THE REPUBLIC'S EARLY DAYS

On January 1, 1804, Dessalines proclaimed the independence of the former French colony at the city of Gonaïves. Saint Domingue resumed its old Indian name of Haiti, and a new nation was born, different from any other at the time—the first independent black state in the New World! As the first ruler of the new nation, Dessalines assumed the title of Emperor and ruled until he was assassinated in 1806, presumably by mulattoes who were terrified by the emergence of a black ruling class.

Following the assassination of Dessalines, one of his black army lieutenants, Henri Christophe, took control of the northern part of the country and established a new capital at Cap-Haïtien, where he proclaimed himself King of Haiti, in 1811. Meanwhile, in the south, the mulattoes had elected one of their own members, Alexandre Pétion, to succeed Dessalines, with the result that the nation was divided. The north was ruled as a monarchy by King Christophe until 1820 and the rest of the country was ruled as a republic by Alexandre Pétion, with his capital at Port-au-Prince.

Christophe governed with an iron hand and during his reign was responsible for the building of the famous Citadelle LaFerrière and the Palace of Sans Souci. Growing more and more tyrannical and less popular with his increasingly rebellious subjects, the Black King suffered a paralyzing stroke while attending church in 1820. Rather than be humiliated before his in-

The mighty fortress of King Christophe, La Citadelle Ferrière, overlooks the little town of Milot near Cap-Haïtien.

On the ramparts of the Citadelle are some of the 365 cannons which were never fired.

surgent subjects he fired a silver bullet into his head. The Citadelle, high up in the mountains, reached only by a mule-track, is an architectural wonder. This great fortress now serves as his burial place, but it may be even more than this, for it may also be the burial place for a treasure of gold and precious stones which the Black King reportedly concealed within the dark confines of the mammoth Citadelle shortly before his death. Today the ruins of Sans Souci, which served during its day as the grand palace for King Christophe, and the famous Citadelle, are among the chief attractions for hardy visitors to the Caribbean.

As ruler of the southern state, Alexandre Pétion, died a natural death in 1818, while still president of his republic. His administration was marked by breaking up the large plantations and distributing the land in small plots to the former slaves, whereby Haiti became a nation of small farmers, which it still is today.

After Pétion's death, Jean Pierre Boyer, was elected president and he ruled for 25 years, assuming jurisdiction over the entire country upon the death of Henri Christophe. During his rule he conquered the eastern end of the island (what we know today as the Dominican Republic). Haiti was to rule over the conquered land for 22 years from 1822 to 1844, when the Dominicans declared their independence from Haiti. There followed a long period of in-stability under various dictators. One of the dictators, Faustin Soulouque, even revived the monarchy and ruled Haiti as Emperor Faustin I from 1848 until 1859.

THE 20TH CENTURY

The dawn of the 20th century found the nation facing many new problems. Gone were the prosperous colonial days, and the vast plantations and prosperous sugar mills that had been destroyed during the long slave rebellion and wars for independence. With Haiti now a nation of small farm owners, the former slaves were content to raise just enough food for their own immediate family use. Most of the people were extremely poor and uneducated and they had no experience whatever in governing themselves. As other Caribbean countries continued to progress and prosper, the economic conditions of Haiti continued to decay, with presidents and dictators coming and going at a faster rate. Revolutions became common events and the deep scars that existed between the black and mulattoes became deeper than before. Soon, the nation was bankrupt, and in political chaos, with its people living in grinding poverty—without adequate food, clothing, housing, health care, education, and above all—without hope of achieving anything better. Such was the dismal picture of Haiti at the start of the 20th century.

In a Mardi Gras procession, pretty girls ride a float dedicated to François Duvalier.

Except for a few short intervals of relative calm, Haiti was in a state of political turmoil throughout most of the first half of the 20th century. In 1915, during a violent political upheaval the United States Marines landed in Haiti, purportedly for the protection of American life and property. The occupation lasted until 1934, during which time the United States made public improvements and bolstered the sagging economy by granting huge loans to the nation. It was also during the years of this occupation that the first trickle of tourists discovered that Haiti was a vacation paradise for sun and pleasure. However, many Haitians resented the occupation as a violation of Haiti's sovereign rights.

Finally, in 1950, the government structure was reorganized under a new constitution which provided for the election of the president by direct popular vote of the people. Paul Magloire was the first president elected in this manner, in 1951, but ugly politics appeared again when he attempted to remain in office at the expiration of his term, which brought about more violence and strife until he was finally evicted by force.

Disregarding the lessons learned during the past, the struggle between the black leaders and the wealthy mulattoes for political supremacy of the nation was renewed again with more bitterness than ever. During the years from 1950 to 1959, five different governmental régimes were toppled from office. Revolutions, street fights, dicatorships and political chaos were fast becoming a way of life. The political dilemma was not to subside until September 22, 1957, when Dr. François Duvalier (Papa Doc), a black conservative country doctor, was elected president of the republic for a term of 6 years.

FRANÇOIS DUVALIER

During 1964, a new constitution was adopted that made the aging Dr. Duvalier president for life. Despite strong opposition to his dictatorial one-man rule, he survived several violent outbreaks against his rule during 1963 and 1970, aided by a much feared corps of secret police known as the Tonton Macoute. The rule of the black president was marked with severe blows to the prestige of the educated and wealthy mulattoes of the nation, who in many cases migrated to other lands. Although the black-oriented government of Dr. Duvalier attempted to make many reforms for the benefit of the poor black population, the régime was filled with an uneasiness and fear that caused tourism to grind to a screeching halt. Wrapped in a blanket of isolation by the black ruler, Haiti soon became the forgotten island of the Caribbean.

Before his death on April 21, 1971, the age-limit requirement to become president was lowered in order that his son, Jean-Claude Duvalier (Baby Doc), age 19, might succeed the ailing doctor as president for life. Despite predictions that the young ruler's régime would be brief—that a bitter, bloody, power struggle would throw the country into deep chaos—this did not happen. To the contrary, exports have increased, tourism has spiralled upward and there are good omens for the future. The initial success of young Duvalier's régime has been attributed to liberal influences from older members of the Duvalier family circle.

Jean-Claude Duvalier succeeded his father as president (for life) of Haiti in 1971.

A picture of Haiti's President, Jean-Claude Duvalier, appears in a park in Port-au-Prince. The French caption reads, "The Haitian People's Idol."

25

Haiti's beautiful "White House," the National Palace—home of Haitian presidents during most of this century—rises against a background of green mountains.

3. GOVERNMENT

THE CONSTITUTION under which Haiti has been governed since 1964 includes 201 articles, with the usual democratic provisions that divide the powers of the government among the legislative, executive and judicial branches.

EXECUTIVE

The executive power is vested in the president, with power to hold office for life. Under the constitution the president is vested with great powers, including the right to dissolve the legislature and govern by decree in cases of emergency. The president is also the commander-in-chief of the Haitian armed forces, comprising an army, air corps and coast guard with a combined total strength of about 6,000 men. Military service is obligatory. Officers of the army, air corps and navy—which consists of a number of coast guard vessels—are trained in the Military Academy of Haiti, most of whose instructors are graduates of military academies of the United States or France.

The president also directly commands an additional paramilitary civilian militia—an active reserve of armed governmental partisans (including women) with nominal military training and organization. In addition to this,

Haiti's Legislative Palace, or Congress Building, is one of a number of new structures that contrast sharply with the older buildings of Port-au-Prince.

the president heads an élite military force, the "Leopards," who replace the Tonton Macoute, which was dissolved in 1971.

LEGISLATIVE

The legislative branch is composed of a single-chamber National Assembly with 58 deputies elected by the people to serve for a term of 6 years. Prior to 1961, the legislature was bicameral (two-chambered) with a Chamber of Deputies and a Senate. Haitian legislation is largely modelled on French law. There is only one legal political party, the Parti Unité Nationale, and all 58 legislators belong to it.

JUDICIARY

The judicial branch is composed of the Court of Cassation, which may rule on the actions of lower courts; courts of appeal, civil tribunals or tribunals of the first instance, and justices of the peace. The judges are named by the president of the republic, subject to certain conditions laid down by law. Judges of the Court of Cassation and courts of appeal serve for 10 years, while judges of civil tribunals are appointed for a term of seven years.

LOCAL GOVERNMENT

The country is divided into 20 local units called prefectures, each headed by an official (prefect) appointed by the president.

NATIONAL FLAG

Haiti's national flag as designated by the constitution of 1964 consists of two vertical stripes, black at the hoist and red at the fly. Superimposed in the middle on a white scroll is the national coat-of-arms with the motto, *L'Union fait la Force* (Union makes Strength).

The National Anthem is "La Dessalinienne."

WORLD AFFILIATIONS

Haiti became a charter member of the United Nations in 1945, and three years later it joined the Organization of American States.

Haitian women pray for help in overcoming the dire poverty of their country, at the religious festival held at Saut d'Eau every July. Pilgrims from all over Haiti flock to the village, where there are both Roman Catholic and voodoo ceremonies. Many Haitians believe the sacred waterfall possesses healing powers.

The din of crowded markets, where the exotic quality of Creole voices may be heard along with the cackle of poultry and the braying of donkeys, adds immeasurably to the charm of Haiti. This busy scene shows one of the downtown shopping streets of Port-au-Prince.

4. THE PEOPLE

WITH NEARLY 5,000,000 people squeezed into a mountainous terrain, Haiti averages more than 445 persons per square mile and ranks among the most densely populated nations in the Western Hemisphere. Since much of the nation's land is wholly unfit for farming, more than 85 per cent of the people are crowded into the overworked agricultural regions of the lowlands and valleys where they toil for a scant subsistence from the eroded soil.

About 90 per cent of native Haitians are pure Negro descendants of slaves who came from Senegal, Ghana, Guinea, the Congo, Dahomey and other African lands. Over the years the folk patterns and ancient beliefs of many tribes from Africa were transplanted to this Caribbean island country, where they have been mixed with the sophisticated culture of the French. The mixture has resulted in a unique race of Christian, but voodoo worshipping, Creole-speaking people, that sets them apart from most Caribbean peoples.

Although poverty and illiteracy are common throughout the island, Haitians have neverthe-

A majority of Haitians are poor peasants with little or no education, living on small farms or in small villages dotting the country. In many respects the poor peasants live a life similar to the peasant farmer in West Africa. This farm scene is typical of many throughout the country.

Under a cactus-like tree, a peasant hut is being built. The walls, of latticed sticks, will be plastered with lime when completed.

Thatched huts like this one are being replaced by more solid houses of stone in many rural areas.

Peasants in rural areas use clean (sometimes unclean) water from rivers and streams to bathe in and do their laundry. However, washday is eagerly looked forward to by the hard-working peasant women, since it affords a time for lively gossip and a chance to catch up on the latest local news.

less, by their instinctive skill, gained world recognition for their style in paintings, wood carving and sculpture, and their own distinctive type of music and dancing. It is remarkable that the Haitians managed to survive three centuries of bloody conquest, and cruel enslavement and emerged from it all as the friendly and happy people which they are today. Even among the poorest folk there prevails an eagerness to live each day up to the hilt—to laugh, sing and dance, with a zest for uninhibited, carefree living, that adds immeasurably to the charm of the island.

STANDARD OF LIVING

A majority of the people are poor peasants with little or no education, who live on small farms or in villages dotting the countryside and lead a rural life similar in many respects to that of the peasant farmer in West Africa. The African influence in the rural sections is very strong. The rural Haitians generally live in one-room huts, made of roughly hewn boards covered with clay and mud, and capped by a roof of palm leaves or straw. Hard-packed earth serves for the floor, where they sleep upon a bed of straw. Crude as the huts may appear, they prove fairly effective in shedding the torrential rains during the rainy season. From one to three families may live in a single hut and the sanitary conditions are often bad.

Resting on her haunches (called "haunching"), an elderly country woman pauses momentarily while doing the family laundry to light her pipe with home-grown tobacco.

The quantity of things that can be carried on the head is often surprising.

This typical hard-working Haitian woman has classical African features.

The average farm consists of no more than 2 or 3 acres ($\frac{3}{4}$ to $1\frac{1}{4}$ hectares) which have been handed down from one generation to the next. Generally the soil is overworked and eroded and farming is done by one or two crude farming tools such as a pointed stick, a shovel and a hoe. Communities, sometimes consisting of just a few families clustered together for safety and convenience, lie scattered across the country, even in the isolated mountains. Drums still serve in the remote areas as a means of communication.

Since the annual per capita income of Haitians is only about U.S. $70, it is obvious that the Haitian farmer earns very little money. Fortunately, the farmer requires but a very small income to live and raise his family. The peasants grow most of their own food which includes such staples as maize, yams, and beans, in addition to the usual wide selection of tropical fruit, especially bananas and plantains. Some peasants own a few chickens, pigs or goats. If a peasant is lucky he may own a mule,

Ice-cream vendors do a brisk business in the warm sunny Haitian markets.

Fermathe, a farm area near the capital, is the site of an agricultural renewal project, where sturdy houses like the one seen here have been built for the farmers.

but few are ever that fortunate. Others work upon large company-owned sugar cane or sisal plantations, and they too live in miserable one-room shacks.

If the members of the family are fortunate enough to raise more food than the family requires, they tote it to one of the local markets for sale or to barter it for other necessities. In Haiti, it is the women who do most of the work and all the "merchandising." Haitian women, gaily dressed, carrying large baskets of farm produce on their heads, often trudge many miles to arrive at a marketplace before dawn. With the money they receive, which is seldom more than a few coins, they buy the few manufactured items they need—cloth for clothing, oil for their lamps or perhaps a few iron cooking utensils.

Family ties and community loyalties are very strong in the rural sections. Peasants frequently band together in *coumbites* or work gangs, to build a house for a man whose house has burned to the ground, or to harvest the crop of one who is ill. The work of a coumbite is invariably done to the accompaniment of rhythmic work songs. When the work is finished the workers celebrate with a *bamboche* or party.

Haitians for the most part are physically

This father and daughter in their Sunday best are more prosperous than the average Haitian.

As one climbs higher in the hills surrounding the capital, tin-can shanties give way to the houses of the élite.

Charming and sophisticated, they identify themselves not with Africa, but with France, where many of them have gone for their education. They much prefer to be called "Creoles," rather than mulattoes. Beneath his hospitality and graciousness, the Haitian Creole inwardly feels superior to Anglo-Saxon and Hispanic Americans.

Today, however, the once proud rulers of Haiti have lost much of their former power. Jean-Claude Duvalier's government is black-directed, black-controlled and the quality of life in government circles is black. While the black-oriented government has not eliminated the Creoles entirely it has reduced many of them to rôles of minor importance.

Of late, there is a noticeable change in the caste structure of Haiti, as a new middle class is beginning to assert itself. Composed mainly of poor black peasants who have used their initiative to forge ahead, they are now pulling themselves up from poverty to become skilled technicians, merchants, doctors, lawyers, nurses and scholars.

strong and notably erect in carriage. The average Haitian is a person of simple dignity, possessing a fierce pride in his heritage and freedom, friendly, good-natured and happy, despite the poverty and illiteracy in which most of the people are forced to exist.

CULTURE AND SOCIAL LIFE

At the opposite end of the social ladder is the small group of mulattoes who have until recent years dominated the political and social scene in Haiti. Centuries of bitter rivalry between the two classes for political and social supremacy has created a deep-seated class distinction that still exists throughout the nation today.

Mulattoes are descendants of early French settlers, with varying admixtures of Negro blood. In number they represent no more than about 3 per cent of Haiti's 5,000,000 population.

At Haiti's Hotel Training School young ladies prepare Haitian specialties—rice and peas, "délicieuse au fromage" (a tasty cheese preparation) and mango pies.

Haiti's architecture is uniquely its own, with features copied from Chinese pagodas, Indian mosques, Norman farmhouses (above) and Victorian gingerbread mansions (below), blended together in a distinctively native manner.

CO. SCHOOLS
C823373

Like some pupils everywhere, these Haitian primary school youngsters must be urged to return to the classroom after recess.

The Technical School at Cap-Haïtien was modernized and reorganized with help of experts from the International Labour Organization.

At Marbial, a rural community, a teacher lectures a class of young people on agricultural methods.

EDUCATION

One of the major handicaps Haiti inherited from the French Colonial era was widespread illiteracy resulting from the total lack of an educational system. The French plantation owners showed very little interest in providing schools for their illiterate black slaves. So it was not until after the bloody slave revolt and Haiti had gained its independence that any effort was made toward establishing an educational system.

Although nearly 90 per cent of the people of Haiti can neither read nor write and school attendance is low, definite progress has been made in combating this national problem. The constitution now provides for compulsory primary education and guarantees that primary and secondary education shall be free to everyone. However, illiteracy and low school attendance in rural areas are difficult to combat because peasant families have traditionally depended upon their school-age children for help in making a livelihood and also because of

Haiti has this modern school of Pharmacy and Medicine at Port-au-Prince, but there is still an acute shortage of doctors.

Carpenters are being trained, along with other technicians, at the J. B. Damier Vocational School in Port-au-Prince.

the lack of transportation to schools in remote areas.

Despite severe handicaps, the Haitian peasants have proven to be eager students as they come to realize that education may be the only means available to pull themselves up from poverty. Today great emphasis is being placed upon the teaching of agriculture, animal husbandry, forestry and technical training.

Haitians are very proud of the University of Haiti, and the schools and institutes affiliated with it, such as the College of Medicine, the College of Dentistry, the School of Pharmacy,

the College of Law, the National School of Agriculture, the Grand Seminaire Notre Dame, designed to train native Catholic priests, the Institute of Ethnology, the School of Surveying, the Polytechnic Institute, and the Superior Normal School for Teachers in secondary schools. Law Schools are established in the cities of Cap-Haïtien, Les Cayes, Jérémie and Gonaïves. In addition, there are numerous Catholic schools and private vocational schools, as well as the Governmental Division of Agriculture Extension schools.

The younger generation are thirsty for learning as evidenced by these girls studying in a city park.

Future nurses of Haiti file into the National School of Nursing in Port-au-Prince.

HEALTH

The life expectancy of the average male in Haiti is only 35 years and health conditions are still very poor. Poor sanitation plagues much of the nation. In rural areas, people are very often forced to use water from rivers that are unclean and only a small part of the urban population is supplied with adequate drinking water. Many Haitians do not receive the variety of foods needed for good health, and suffer from malnutrition; such diseases as tuberculosis and hookworm are common.

Throughout Haiti there is a shortage of doctors and hospitals, with an average of only one physician for about every 10,000 inhabitants. Unfortunately, many of the nation's hospitals and physicians are concentrated in the urban areas, to the disadvantage of the rural population.

In recent years the Ministry of Public Health, working in conjunction with various world health organizations, has made rewarding progress in a war to improve health conditions and reduce disease. Yaws and malaria, two of Haiti's most dreaded diseases, have all but been eradicated, but tuberculosis continues to be a major problem. Many new medical clinics are under construction throughout the nation, especially in the rural areas, but many more will still be needed to cope with the expanding population.

LANGUAGE

Although French is the official language of Haiti almost everyone speaks a rich, soft purring dialect known as Creole—the peasants speak nothing else. About the only occasion on which you will hear pure French spoken is when mingling with the upper crust of Haitian society or dealing with high government officials where the official tongue of Haiti is beautifully spoken.

The Creole patois is a corruption of early 17th-century buccaneer French with African tongues and an infusion of English, Spanish and Indian words. African influence contributed to the suppression of the *r* and *s* sounds and gave the language its accent, modulation and tone. The word Creole, for example, is pronounced *Cweole* by the natives.

The rich patois is full of Haitian proverbs such as "*Che go kat pat, se you sel cheme li te,*" meaning "A dog has four paws, but he can only go one way." In describing the mountains of Haiti, the natives will say "*Deye mon ge mon,*" meaning "Beyond the mountains there are more mountains." And, to mention one of their most popular, "*Ka poul bwe dlo, li pa blie Bo-Die,*" means "When a chicken drinks water it doesn't forget to raise its head in thanks to God."

Modern Creole and French are now both taught in the public schools. English is no

Although voodooism is widespread, Haiti has many beautiful churches, since the official religion of Haiti is Roman Catholic. This church still displays pictures of the late "Papa Doc" on either side of the door.

The African word voodoo means "god," "spirit," or "sacred object." Often misunderstood by foreigners, voodooism has nothing to do with "black magic," but is in fact a true folk religion invoking the spirits of ancestors, African gods, and Christian saints. Essentially voodooism holds that the Supreme Being is unconcerned with the problems of mankind, but can be reached through a group of lower deities known as *loas*, among which are Legba, guardian of temples; Erzulie, goddess of love; Ogoun, god of war; and Agoué, lord of the sea.

An authentic voodoo ceremony with animal sacrifices is not for the squeamish and it is rarely witnessed by outsiders. Generally, a voodoo ceremony takes place in the *houmfor*, which is a hut with a palm-thatched or tin roof,

longer the strange foreign language in Haiti that it used to be, since it is now a mandatory subject in the public schools. The English-speaking visitor to Haiti will find that English is spoken in Port-au-Prince by most hotel managers and people working in shops and in connection with the tourist industry. English is also spoken to a lesser extent in all the provincial cities of any size at hotels and tourist attractions. Along the Dominican border a Spanish Creole is spoken.

RELIGION

The official religion is Roman Catholicism, but Haiti has freedom of worship and a number of Protestant sects have a growing membership. However, unique in the realm of religion is the ancient worship of voodoo (*voudou* in French) now found almost exclusively in Haiti where, in spite of official strictures against it by the Catholic Church, it continues to flourish.

Near the middle of Port-au-Prince, the famous Basilica of Notre Dame displays its sober but imposing Romanesque architecture.

Murmuring and chanting in Creole, a high priest weaves a mystic pattern of cornmeal (called a "vêver") upon the floor, a preliminary rite performed before a complex voodoo ceremony.

half-open to the warm night air. The ceremony begins with a prayer or tuneful invocation and this is followed by rites called the *Yanvalou,* the *Voodoo,* and the *Congo,* ending with a cheerful air— the *Banda.* The ceremony is conducted by a high priest called a *houngan* or by a priestess known as a *mambo,* assisted by lesser priests, called variously *hounsis, hounguenicons, laplaces,* and *boulattiers.*

During the ceremony there are prayers and songs to every loa, and to be in communication with the god, the Haitian must become "possessed" by the spirit of his loa. Possession by the loa is induced mainly by the drummers who beat out a hypnotic rhythm with such intensity of percussion that the frenzied singers often go into a trance and fall to the floor completely exhausted. This is taken to mean that the worshipper is "possessed' by the loa—the god has actually entered his body and soul.

Many Haitian practitioners of voodoo do not understand the full meaning of the complex ritual ceremonies themselves. Perhaps it is just as well since it serves them, just as it served their slave ancestors, with an opportunity to forget their hardships and their poverty, if only for a very short while.

Visitors to Haiti determined to view a voodoo ceremony will find a number of places, night clubs and hotels, featuring sensual "rites" adapted from the actual voodoo religion. The

A voodoo ceremony is performed for tourists on the outskirts of Port-au-Prince.

An aged drummer thumps out the voodoo beat for the benefit of tourists.

FOLKLORE AND MUSIC

Haiti is one of the most fascinating of all Caribbean countries from the standpoint of music and African folklore. In fact, the African influence has been so faithfully preserved throughout the country that present-day songs and dances differ little from those of the slave period of centuries ago.

In the vast repertory of original folk songs is a song for every occasion. Most of the songs are not lyrical at all, but chants, seldom in harmony, but sung according to the mood and feeling of the singer at the time.

In addition to the voodoo ritual songs there are also many other types, among which are the work songs of the *coumbite,* which are sung by the workers in a lively tempo and often spiced with gossip.

Other songs expressing happiness are the party songs sung at the *bamboche* and during the Mardi Gras. Still other songs recite a story or

version seen by tourists may not be authentic, but it is usually a unique and exciting spectacle that helps to make a visit to Haiti a memorable occasion.

The Théâtre de Verdure, at Port-au-Prince, presents regular open-air performances by dance troupes and other entertainers.

"La Danse d'Araignée" (The Spider Dance) is an African dance seldom seen by visitors.

A voodoo drummer beats out the heady rhythms of African Haiti.

Performers do a traditional Creole dance, in the costume of colonial times.

Various government ministries (Finance, Economic Affairs) are represented by this Mardi Gras float.

A lively native band is generally on hand to greet visitors arriving at the François Duvalier Airport at Port-au-Prince.

Cock fighting is one of the passions of Haitians, who find it a way to pass a rousing Sunday afternoon.

memorialize an outstanding event. Others, like the song written by Othelo Bayard, entitled "Haïti Chéri" (Beloved Haiti) tenderly and poetically express the deep love of Haitians for their homeland.

The chief musical instrument of Haiti is the drum, which comes in a wide variety of sizes and shapes. However, many Haitians are gifted with the art of picking a "hot guitar" or squeezing an accordion. When a group of Haitian musicians gather for a peasant party, the music that ensues can be heard nowhere but in Haiti. Conch shells (called *lambis*) are sometimes used to bring out the bass notes that Haitians love so well to hear.

The national dance of Haiti is the *meringue* (or *merengue*) which is also called the wooden leg dance because it is executed by holding one leg stiff and gyrating the pelvic joint and kneecap of the other leg. The dance is not only popular in Haiti but with ballroom dancers in many other countries.

The natural grace of Haitians is clearly reflected in their lithe dancing, in which the peasants dance individually rather than cheek to cheek. Their uninhibited hip swaying and gyrating body motions, always to the rhythmic beat of hypnotic drums, is their way of expressing their happiness and joy of living.

MARDI GRAS

One of the most exciting events in all the Caribbean is Haiti's famous Mardi Gras which generally takes place in late February or early March. The traditional carnival is made up by the people themselves rather than by commercial interest. The scores of elaborate floats that parade are full of symbolism and magic. Colorful costumes are inspired by Haiti's historical past—some grotesque, some beautiful— but even the grotesque are colorful and beautiful. The festival lasts from three to four days with the grand finale taking place at the Presidential Palace where the king and beautiful queen of the Mardi Gras receive a warm welcome by the President himself.

OTHER HOLIDAYS

January 1 in Haiti is not only New Year's Day, but also Independence Day, and thus is a doubly joyous event. The chief religious holidays are Christmas, All Saints' Day (November 1), and the Feasts of the Ascension (May 19), and the Assumption (August 15). Non-religious holidays include the Anniversary of the death of Dessalines (October 17) and Labor Day (May 1).

45

Art blossoms everywhere in Haiti, not only in paintings and wood carvings but in clothing and dance. The artists through oils and brushes, through simple carving knives, awls and hand drills, can truly put "soul" into objects depicting everyday life, rural village scenes, tragedy, gaiety and toil. "Earthly Paradise," (seen here) is an oil painting by the internationally famous Haitian artist, Wilson Biguad.

Shops in Haiti offer a wide variety of objects crafted from wood—everything from drums to masks, pestles and statues.

Ceramics is a relatively new "small industry" in Haiti. Here a craftsman places various ceramic objects in the furnace to be fired.

These young men are patiently hand polishing wooden bowls for exports.

ARTS AND CRAFTS

Haiti enjoys an enviable reputation throughout the world for its vivid paintings and fine sculpture. The "renaissance" of Haitian painting started during 1944 when an American artist and school teacher, DeWitt Peters, opened the Centre d'Art in Port-au-Prince, for the purpose of encouraging the art movement. The response was great from the very beginning as hundreds of illiterate, untrained, beginners poured forth from the mountains and city slums to take their very first lesson in oil painting. Three years later, under Peters' expert eye, the first Haitian "primitive" paintings received an enthusiastic reception at the re-

Artist Bevott Castre has his own "sidewalk" art studio near the city wharf of Port-au-Prince.

Haitian sculptors put hours of painstaking skill into their mahogany carvings, which may be purchased at modest prices.

In Port-au-Prince, the city of contrasts, a modern sculpture stands out against the severe white façade of the building in the background.

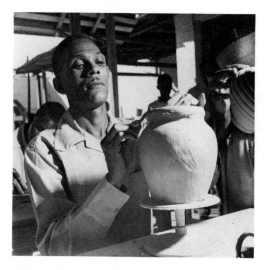

This ceramicist shows total concentration as he moulds a large urn by hand.

nowned International Exhibition in Paris. By 1949, Haitian primitive paintings were demanding top prices in the large art galleries of New York City.

During the same year the American poet and art critic, Selden Rodman, launched the mural movement in paintings. Within a short time Haitian artists were painting huge murals in the church cathedrals, and on the walls of hotels, airport and exposition buildings, until these largely self-taught artists became household names in the art world. The most magnificent of these giant murals may be seen today in the Episcopal Cathedral of the Holy Trinity at Port-au-Prince.

Among Haiti's renowned artists, are the late Hector Hyppolite, who during his life was also a voodoo priest; Wilson Bigaud, the first Haitian to exhibit his paintings at the Carnegie

Artistic hand-carved wooden masks occasionally are used by revellers during carnival.

Woodcraft forms one of Haiti's most important exports. This man is carefully sanding a wooden bowl by hand.

International; Philomé Obin and Enguerrang Gourge, whose paintings are among those included in the permanent collection of New York's Museum of Modern Art.

Some of Haiti's prominent artists are now painting in more modern forms, but their paintings still retain a pronounced African touch to make them recognizable as pure Haitian, prized by art collectors throughout the world.

The visitor will find that Port-au-Prince is an art buyer's paradise with many excellent art galleries lining the narrow streets, where the paintings on sale reflect the ingenuity and refinement of a remarkable people.

In this original oil painting, the artist, J. Innocent, tells the story of some peasants as they work their small sugar mill.

49

Fishing boats crowd the waterfront at Port-au-Prince.

Oxen cool off in an irrigation ditch while their carts are being loaded with sugar cane.

5. THE ECONOMY

AFTER MORE THAN a century and a half of independence, Haiti still suffers a material poverty unequalled anywhere else in the Caribbean. The economic condition of the nation has never come close to approaching the great prosperity of the 18th century when, as a French colony, Haiti became the most productive land of the Caribbean.

The first cause of economic decay came during the bloody slave revolution of 1791, when the revolting slaves slaughtered thousands of French colonists and plundered the wealth-producing sugar plantations and mills established by the French. Following the slave rebellion and the long war with France there followed a complete transformation of the colonial economic system from one of vast productive plantations worked by slaves to a national economy in which the large plantations were broken up into thousands of small individually owned farms, barely capable of supporting their owners.

A worker in the cane fields rinses his hands in an irrigation canal.

Harvesting sugar cane by hand is hard work. Mechanized agriculture is still far from the rule in Haiti.

The cane in this field is headed for a mill where it will be made into "clairin," an intoxicating drink.

Sisal grows well in the coastal lowlands, which receive little rainfall and are often very hot. After being harvested, the sisal, which then looks like shorn locks of long blond hair, will be processed in a Haitian factory.

A United Nations weaving expert helps a student to set a pattern on a small hand loom. This type of loom is used to make mats from sisal, royal palm fibre or cotton.

AGRICULTURE

Farming, now as in the past, is the mainstay of the Haitian economy, with about 90 per cent of the population depending upon the soil for a living. A small percentage of the land is farmed by sharecroppers, while only about 10 per cent of the land is operated as well run mechanized sugar cane or sisal plantations.

Coffee is the most important commercial crop raised for export and at times it accounts for as much as three fourths of total export sales. Sisal, a plant used for making twine and rope, is an important agricultural product in the drier areas. Sugar cane is grown mostly by large corporations engaged only in the making of sugar for export. Other products raised by the peasants include rice, cacao (used to make chocolate), tobacco, the much used calabash (gourd), breadfruit, mango, maize and a wide variety of citrus fruits and nuts. In addition, there is some stock raising which seems to meet most of the domestic demands. Animal husbandry has recently been upgraded by the government and there are now two stock-

Haiti is famous for the high quality of its rum. Here an original authentic mule-driven sugar cane mill is on display at the famous Barancourt Rum Factory near Port-au-Prince.

A housewife at Fermathe near Port-au-Prince proudly displays fruit grown on her family plot, with aid from the United Nations Technical Assistance Administrator.

Large numbers of fish ponds have been installed in different parts of Haiti in an effort to increase the protein supply. Here United Nations experts count fish just taken from a pond for inspection.

breeding stations in operation at Port-au-Prince and at Cap-Haïtien.

Faced with the big problem of feeding an ever rapidly increasing population upon the limited amount of arable soil available, the government is attempting to meet the chal-

This little fish is a young tilapia, one of the food fishes being bred in Haitian ponds.

Haiti has many small plantations where tobacco is grown mostly for export.

Sisal, which grows well in arid regions, has been planted on eroded slopes as a cover crop.

The dam at Péligre has been built to provide hydro-electric power for all of Haiti.

A new fish pond is under way as workers remove soil for the pond bed.

Under the reorganized Haitian Forestry Service, foresters are being trained in the conservation of Haiti's woodlands.

assembled by Haitian workers at very low cost. The finished product is then shipped back to the high-priced markets.

Haiti has a number of trade unions, but as yet they do not carry much weight. However, in industry and service operations the 8-hour day and 2-week paid vacation are standard.

TRANSPORTION

Transportation to the interior of Haiti is handicapped by the mountainous nature of the island. The nation has scarcely more than 400 miles (640 km.) of main highways and about 1,500 miles (2,400 km.) of secondary roads, some of which are utterly impassable except by mule and foot during the rainy seasons.

lenge by completing the dam at Péligre which will provide cheap hydro-electric power for most of the nation and will reclaim thousands of acres of desert land for arable farming lands.

INDUSTRY AND WAGES

Haiti welcomes and greatly needs any kind of new industry that will provide work for its inhabitants. United States investments in Haiti currently amount to approximately U.S. $50,000,000, mostly in mining and power, sugar mills, meat processing and packing, petroleum products and certain assembly operations.

Recently there has been a marked growth of light industries in the capital, particularly in producing articles for export. An abundant supply of manpower, both skilled and unskilled, has encouraged the importing of components from North America and having the parts

A small rice paddy with its crop of precious grain swaying in the breeze is a common sight in the southern coastal region. Rice and beans combine to form the national dish of Haiti.

Large steel beams for a nearby construction project block sidewalk traffic in front of the City Hall of Port-au-Prince.

Haiti's hustling Chamber of Commerce has been very instrumental in attracting new industries to the republic.

Skilled carpenters nail forms in place to mould cement that will be mixed and poured by hand.

Huge freighters and passenger vessels are familiar sights along the waterfront of Port-au-Prince.

If it can be carried at all, Haitians will carry it on their heads. In this case the customary basket has been replaced by an inverted chair.

A giant carving from a tree root dominates the hall of the François Duvalier Airport, inaugurated on September 22, 1967. The largest jet planes can come into this airport.

Feeder roads from farm to markets are few and most of the produce for the local markets is transported by donkey or carried on the heads of the peasant women. Haiti's best and main road is a two-lane, partially paved highway that stretches for 200 miles (320 km.) through the mountains connecting the capital of Port-au-Prince with Cap-Haïtien on the north coast. The nation has several small railways, but they are used mostly for freight.

The ports of the leading cities are excellent. A fleet of small sailing vessels and a few motor vessels of light tonnage serve the coastal trade. Service with foreign countries is provided by a

Haiti is a nation without true passenger railways. Nevertheless, this mini-size freight engine, running daily, blocks traffic in front of the City Hall at Port-au-Prince.

Mass confusion reigns early each morning at the Port-au-Prince open air bus depot when the heavily laden buses leave for all parts of the nation. Not infrequently, cackling chickens, small pigs and goats are forced to endure the long trips along with the passengers, on the hard wooden benches.

number of foreign shipping lines plus pleasure cruise ships that make the capital and Cap-Haïtien regular stops.

International air service is provided by several leading world airline companies. Domestic air service is supplied by the government operated airline (COHATA), which connects principal cities on regular flight schedules. Bus service throughout the nation is plentiful and cheap, but the overland *camion* (bus), with hard wooden bench seats, are used almost entirely by the peasants.

FOREIGN TRADE AND FINANCE

Coffee ranks as the most important export, followed by sisal. However, sisal exports have been on the decline as export of sugar, cacao, molasses, rum, cotton, tobacco, turpentine, paint and essential oils continues to increase.

During 1964, about 62,000 metric tons (68,200 tons) of sugar and 2,500 metric tons (2,750 tons) of cacao were produced for export, which has increased year after year.

Bauxite is the main mineral export followed by copper. Beautiful hand-carved figures of wood and other handicrafts, along with the native oil paintings, have become a source of revenue in recent years.

Imports for the most part consist of textiles, clothing, chemicals, petroleum, minerals, cars, hardware items and mechanical goods. The bulk of Haiti's foreign trade is with the United States.

Haiti's financial system is controlled by a system that was established during the year 1915, when, by treaty, the United States undertook to reorganize Haiti's sagging economy. As a result, the National Bank of Haiti (Banque

The traditional outdoor Haitian market sometimes loses the race to progress and is replaced by a complicated system of bays and aisles, freezers and clanging cash registers, as inside this supermarket in Pétionville.

Nationale de la République d'Haïti) became the sole bank of issue and now serves as the official treasury of the government.

The basic monetary unit of Haiti is the *gourde,* which is exchangeable at the legal rate of five gourdes to one dollar (U.S.). United States currency circulates freely throughout the country.

In keeping with the Haitian trend toward modern architecture is the Office of Contributions, where Haitian taxes are collected.

Little Europe—opposite the Port-au-Prince City Hall—is not swanky but is actually quite a large store where one can find practically anything at free-port prices.

An hour's ride by boat from Port-au-Prince, Sandy Cay Reef provides one of the world's best underwater panoramas for skin divers.

At the famous Cabane Choucoune night club at Pétionville, visitors often join in the lively native dances of Haiti.

Haiti is taking a new look at tourism as a profitable industry that must be developed by building facilities such as Castlehaiti Hotel, located in the cool mountains on the outskirts of Port-au-Prince.

TOURISM

Haiti's tourist trade made great strides from 1953 through 1956 to become one of the principal sources of Haitian revenue. After 1956, however, economic and political upheavals under Doc Duvalier's government and differences between Haiti and the Dominican Republic, caused a sharp decline in the tourist industry.

Haiti has luxury hotels, some of which rank with the most modern in the world. Haitian foods are French and Creole or a combination of both and all are good.

Port-au-Prince is a free port for a wide variety of European specialties that may be purchased at bargain prices. However, the tourist will undoubtedly while away many hours visiting Haiti's own wood factories—watching in fascination at the skill of the wood-carvers at work—or if it is art, to watch over the shoulder of Haitian artists as they bring to life on canvas their bold and imaginative paintings which are often quite modestly priced.

The grand climax of all Haitian visits is to Cap-Haïtien to visit the astonishing architectural wonder—Henri Christophe's Citadelle. Thrusting skyward from a 3,000-foot-high mountain peak the fortress was erected by the black emperor as an impregnable defence against the hated French armies should they ever return to enslave the Haitians. Legend relates that 200,000 workers toiled 13 years to build the enormous fortress designed to garrison 10,000 troops with enough supplies to last for 5 years. Although more than 20,000 workers died from exhaustion during its construction, not a single one of its 365 cannons was ever fired.

At the base of the mountain stands the eerie ruins of Sans Souci Palace, the grandiose structure built for the use of the black king as his private court. Even today, in its ruins, the monumental structure quickens the pulse and stirs the imagination.

HAITI

UNIQUE IN THE *Caribbean*

Haiti's Chamber of Commerce feels that it can justifiably say that the country is unique in the Caribbean.

INDEX